PURE Fred

Rupert Fawcett invented Fred six years ago and both their lives have taken off since then. Rupert has got married and become a father while Fred has become something of a star with books and merchandise published in several countries and an animated TV series currently in production. Fred's past life is documented in Rupert's six previous books, *Fred*, *More Fred*, *The Extraordinary World of Fred*, *The Continued Adventures of Fred*, *Carry on Fred* and *At Home with Fred*. Nowadays Fred can be seen every week in the *Mail on Sunday*.

Pure Fred contains sixty-one new illustrations showing Fred in a variety of bizarre situations with the charming Penelope and the faithful black cat, Anthony.

PURE
Fred

Rupert Fawcett

HEADLINE

FRED AND PENELOPE ALWAYS
PROVIDED THEIR GUESTS WITH
AFTER-DINNER ENTERTAINMENT

FRED HAD HEARD THAT PIP
WAS FOND OF FAST FOOD

FRED AND PENELOPE LIKED TO END
·THE DAY WITH A NICE GLASS
OF WARM MILK

PIP WISHED HE HAD NEVER AGREED TO
HELP FRED WITH THE PRUNING

FRED AND PENELOPE LOVED TO GET
OUT INTO THE COUNTRY AND
STRETCH THEIR LEGS

PENELOPE COULDN'T HELP FEELING
THAT FRED WASN'T ENTERING
INTO THE TRUE SPIRIT OF
THE ADVENTURE HOLIDAY

FRED HAD BEEN LOOKING FORWARD TO
TRYING HIS NEW FIRE EXTINGUISHER

FRED AND PENELOPE LOVED A
TRADITIONAL BRITISH SUMMER TEA :
EARL GREY, STRAWBERRIES AND CREAM
AND CUCUMBER SANDWICHES

'NO PEACE FOR THE WICKED',
SIGHED FRED

FOR MANY YEARS FRED'S SECRET SUNDAY
AFTERNOON NAPS WENT UNDETECTED

FRED AND PENELOPE'S GUESTS
COULD ALWAYS BE SURE OF
A WARM WELCOME

EVERYBODY WAS ASKED TO WAIT
PATIENTLY FOR THEIR TURN WITH
THE SCATTER CUSHIONS

HAVING BEEN UNABLE TO OBTAIN A LION,
FRED SETTLED FOR THE SLIGHTLY LESS
DANGEROUS PURSUIT OF SLUG-TAMING

PENELOPE WAS RELIEVED THAT FRED
HAD AT LAST AGREED TO ATTEND
`ROAD-RAGE` COUNSELLING

AFTER WEEKS OF SCORCHING WEATHER
FRED AND PIP FINALLY DECIDED TO
SHAKE OFF THEIR STUFFY BRITISH
IMAGE AND 'GO MEDITERRANEAN'

FRED'S BIRTHDAY PARTY WAS A SMALL
BUT HAPPY OCCASION

FRED DERIVED IMMENSE PLEASURE
FROM SITTING IN THE BATH FOR
EXTENDED PERIODS AND WATCHING
EVERYTHING GO WRINKLY

IF FRED AND PENELOPE'S FIRST B+B
CUSTOMER HAD ONE COMPLAINT, IT
WOULD SIMPLY BE THAT THEY WERE
TRYING A LITTLE TOO HARD

FRED HAD PROMISED TO GET
MR AND MRS NESBIT HOME IN TIME
FOR THE ARCHERS

AFTER LUNCH FRED TREATED HIS
CHRISTMAS GUESTS TO AN INDOOR
FIREWORK DISPLAY

PENELOPE WAS BEGINNING TO WISH
SHE HAD NEVER BOUGHT FRED
THE CAMCORDER

HAVING GROWN BORED WITH SLUG-TAMING
FRED DECIDED TO TRY HIS HAND
AT WORM-CHARMING

FRED WAS LOOKING FORWARD TO
SEEING HIS LONG-LOST COUSIN

WHAT PENELOPE LIKED MOST ABOUT
LIFE WITH FRED WAS THAT THERE WAS
NEVER A DULL MOMENT

FRED AND PIP WERE THE KINDA GUYS
THAT LIKED TO WORK HARD
AND PLAY HARD

FRED AND PENELOPE SPENT
MANY HAPPY EVENINGS RE-LIVING
THEIR HONEYMOON IN VENICE

PIP SHOULD HAVE KNOWN BETTER
THAN TO MONOPOLISE FRED'S
FAVOURITE ARMCHAIR

ALTHOUGH EVERYBODY LOVED FRED
THEY EACH HAD THEIR OWN
FAVOURITE BIT

PENELOPE FOUND HERSELF WONDERING
WHY SHE HADN'T SIMPLY GONE TO
HER CHIROPODIST APPOINTMENT
BY BUS

WE CALL IT 'ACUTE SOAP ADDICTION
SYNDROME' WHISPERED THE DOCTOR

CONSTANCE GENEROUSLY OFFERED
TO HELP PENELOPE GET FRED TO
HIS DENTAL APPOINTMENT

ONCE OR TWICE A YEAR FRED GOT
TOGETHER WITH HIS OLD SCHOOL
PALS, 'BEAKY' BALDWIN, 'SMARMY'
SMITH AND 'EMBARRASSING' ED

AT LAST PENELOPE FOUND THE
PERFECT WAY TO KEEP FIT,
'VIRTUAL AEROBICS'

FRED AND PENELOPE FREQUENTLY
GOT LOST BETWEEN THE
KITCHEN AND THE LOUNGE

PENELOPE SOMETIMES WISHED FRED PUT
AS MUCH ENERGY INTO THEIR MARRIAGE
AS HE DID INTO HIS HOBBIES

ON THE FIRST DAY OF HIS NEW JOB
FRED EXPERIENCED A FEW
TEETHING PROBLEMS

FRED THOUGHT A LITTLE MUSIC
MIGHT SOOTHE PENELOPE'S MIGRAINE

FRED AND PENELOPE WERE NEVER
AT THEIR BEST FIRST THING
IN THE MORNING

'I THINK THEY CALL IT THE MALE
MENOPAUSE', WHISPERED PENELOPE

THE VALUE OF FRED'S FAMILY
HEIRLOOMS WAS MORE SENTIMENTAL
THAN FINANCIAL

WITH REGULAR VISITS TO THE PET
CEMETERY FRED WAS GRADUALLY
COMING TO TERMS WITH THE
LOSS OF HIS ANT

PENELOPE WAS PLEASED TO SEE
THAT FRED WAS FINALLY TAKING
THE JOB-HUNTING SERIOUSLY

FRED WAS DETERMINED TO PROVE THE
EXISTENCE OF THE MONSTER

WHEN IT CAME TO GARDENING
FRED AND PENELOPE MADE
A GREAT TEAM

FRED WAS DISAPPOINTED TO SEE A
TRUSTED FRIEND BREAKING THE RULES

FRED AND PENELOPE'S SKATING
PARTIES HAD BECOME A
POPULAR CHRISTMAS EVENT

PENELOPE THOUGHT SHE COULD DETECT
THE TELL-TALE SIGNS OF A
MID-LIFE CRISIS

FRED AND PENELOPE TRIED VARIOUS
WAYS OF MAKING THE WALK TO
THE LIBRARY MORE INTERESTING

FRED REALISED HE HAD MADE A
BIG MISTAKE BY CALLING
PENELOPE 'CUDDLY'

'HE'S FAILED TO MAKE THE HONOURS
LIST AGAIN', SIGHED PENELOPE

FRED AND PENELOPE SENSED THAT
THIS WAS NO ORDINARY MOUSE

PENELOPE FINALLY DECIDED TO
DO SOMETHING ABOUT FRED'S
OVER-SLEEPING PROBLEM

FRED COULDN'T HELP FEELING THAT
PENELOPE HAD BOUGHT HIS BIRTHDAY
PRESENT WITH HER OWN USE IN MIND

WHEN IT CAME TO KNITTED MITTENS
AND TEA COSIES MRS NESBIT
REALLY KICKED ASS

FRED AND PIP SEEMED TO HAVE
BECOME A LOT CLOSER SINCE
PIP'S LOTTERY WIN

FRED DIDN'T SETTLE INTO HIS
NEW JOB IMMEDIATELY

IT LOOKED LIKE IT WAS GOING
TO BE 'ONE OF THOSE DAYS'

FRED BELIEVED THERE WERE THREE
IMPORTANT WORDS IN COOKERY ;
PRESENTATION , PRESENTATION
AND PRESENTATION

PENELOPE SOMETIMES WISHED FRED
WOULD GET SOME NORMAL FRIENDS